The **POWER** *of* VISION

APOSTLE DAVID MOSES

ABOUT THE BOOK

In this masterpiece inspired by the Holy Ghost, comes a revolutionary, impactful and powerful revelation titled "The Power Of Vision". The author left no stone unturned as he pours his heart on every page taking us into the mind of God about vision. This book is written for everyone; Pastors, world leaders, sportsmen, Businessmen, Politicians, etc. The style is simple as the author with a keen researcher's mind has been able to draw examples from different sphere of life supported with his vast knowledge of the scriptures.

In this book, you will know:

1. What the meaning of vision is and what true vision entails.

2. How great men and women succeeded on the platform of vision

3. How to understand the timing of vision.

4. How to put your life on the right track via vision.

5. How to achieve greatness and succeed in your every endeavour.

CONTENTS

ACKNOWLEDGMENT

First and foremost, I would like to thank my darling and precious jewel of inestimable value, my wife; Loveth Moses, for standing beside me throughout my career and writing this book. She has been my inspiration and motivation for continuing to improve my knowledge and move my career in ministry forward. She is my rock, and I dedicate this book to her. I also thank my wonderful children: Davidson, Emmanuel, Richard and Chidimma.

I will like to appreciate my Father in the Lord; Rev'd John Ezeh, thank you for nurturing me spiritually, behold the seed you have planted has started yielding bumper harvest for the Lord. Am sure God is proud of you!

I will like to appreciate my mentors for the different roles they have played in my life and ministry; Bishop David Oyedepo, of Winners Chapel and Pastor E. A. Adeboye, of the Redeemed Christian Church Of God. Your messages and exemplary life style mixed with various godly counsel and instruction has birthed a world-wide ministry that is making impact in nations of the world. Thank you for obeying divine mandate.

I will like to thank Pastor Roland and Judith Magaji for their support throughout my years of pain and their trust in my leadership, for without them, I would not have the courage to press on for this book, thank you for your unflinching support, my God will bless you immensely.

I will like to thank all the members of Lighthouse Assembly International Church for their unswerving support, trust and their courage in helping me bring this dream to the world, without you there will be no reason for this seed that has grown into a mighty oak, you are the reason I do what I do, you are the best anywhere in the world and together we will get to the top!

I'd really like to thank Apostle Success Samuel Haruna for providing me with the opportunity to become the lead author for this book. I appreciate that he believed in me to provide the leadership and knowledge to make this book a reality. Apostle Success is a great person, without him, this book may not have been written.

To 'YOU' - My Maker, My Source, My Lord, My Essence, My Life, My King: you invested your treasure in this earthen vessel and made me what I am today. Thank you for counting me worthy for this noble cause and to give me the inspiration to write this book. I appreciate you for all you have done for me and for what you are still prepared to do in and through me. I pledge my undying and unflinching commitment to you my King!

FOREWORD

Without vision people perish.
With vision people flourish.

One of the greatest gift of God to man is the gift of
vision: the blessing of being able to see the beauty of
creation or the dangers that lurk around the corner
with the natural eyes is priceless, how much more is
the ability to psychologically and spiritually visualize
the road ahead and even the destination before you
even start the journey. This kind of vision gives the
ability to navigate without much mistakes and helps
to stay on course to the desired destination.

In this book Apostle David Moses defines the power,
the source and the importance of true vision. He
emphasizes that if one is to avoid the slippery slopes
of social, economical, spiritual and moral decline that
leads to the destination of destruction, he/she must
seek to be a visionary.

Apostle Moses particularly emphasizes the
importance of vision in a leader, inferring that a
leader is not only going somewhere but he is also
taking people somewhere. It is therefore absolutely

imperative that he knows where he is going and how to get there. David showed that a visionary leader is driven by his vision and that it is the vision that helps such leaders to forge ahead in their pursuit where others fizzle out.

Throughout the pages of this book Apostle Moses provides a practical guide to those who have a desire to go somewhere but do not have the vision, insight or tenacity to get there. He passionately expresses his personal belief in the importance of true vision using biblical examples and personalities to authenticate his perspective and belief.

I am confident that everyone who will read and apply the contents of this important book on the "Power of Vision" will enter into a higher dimension of wisdom, power and enlightenment in the quest excellence and success in this life and subsequently in the life to come.

Bishop Dr. Al Baxter Bsc. DD PhD.
Faith Miracle Temple of Toronto Inc.
Faith Missionary Ministries Intl.

DEDICATION

To my lovely wife: LOVETH MOSES, this is for you, I hope it makes you proud!

To my wonderful kids: Daddy has done it again, you will grow up to learn valuable lessons from this piece.

To the entire congregation of LIGHTHOUSE ASSEMBLY INTERNATIONAL: be guided.

To the emerging leaders: this is for you, read through this book many times over, until you can discover your vision and become what god has designed you to be.

INTRODUCTION

In this age and dispensation, when the pursuit of fame and recognition seem to be the yardstick for achieving true success and fulfilment; it becomes imperative for the church to understand true success from God's perspective and how to achieve it. Hence, the need for this masterpiece inspired by the Holy Ghost for this generation.

Vision is an all important subject that everyone who is stern about leaving his footprints in the sands of time must understand and go in pursuit of. The ability to see a glorious future in the midst of gloom and murkiness is what vision entails. It is the ability to see light when you are surrounded with thick darkness. It spurs you into taking steps that will advance your life into the original plan of the master for your life.

Destruction becomes a reality where vision is lacking, because where there is no vision, people perish. It stands to reason that vision can preserve a man's life from despair, misery, hopelessness, despondency and utter destruction.

Every great achievement ever recorded under the sun was made possible because vision was given a chance. No achievement is possible without vision. The colour of man's destiny is determined by the vision he carries. A nation whose leadership lacks vision will have no direction for the destiny of its people, they will fall for anything and make no significant impact on the people or the state because they don't have what it takes to ride to glory and honour.

Even though Abraham was called and blessed as it were in Genesis 12, yet God had to take him go through a training process to appreciate the place of vision. God knew that Abraham's true success lies in his ability to be able to align his sight with God's plan for his life. So when Lot was gone from Abraham, God began to teach Abraham how to take delivery of his promises and prophecies via the instrumentality of vision. "And the Lord said unto Abram, after that Lot was separated from him, lift up now thine eyes and look from the place where thou art northward, and southward, and eastward, and westward: for all the land which thou SEEST, to thee will I give it and to thy seed forever." Genesis 13:14-15

The deal was to see (vision) then you can possess. It is impossible to take possession of what you have not seen. He told Jeremiah "...thou hast well seen: for i will hasten my word to perform it." Jeremiah 1:12. God's word backs up only what you have seen.

Vision is central in the pursuit of success and fulfilment, it is the foundation of every great achievement that is celebrated today in the world. To live life without a vision is to live without worth. No human being can survive without breath so also no destiny can survive without vision.

Vision is the compass you need to navigate through in the journey of life. If you must successfully overcome all the bumps and the contour on your path in life, then you must have vision: in a summary, vision is the unfolding of God's plan for your life. As you read this book, I have no doubt in my mind that you will encounter God on each page. Every page has the potential to turn your life around and inspire a new zeal in you that will take you to the pinnacle of success and the zenith of your life.

1 Where There Is No Vision

Where there is no vision, the people perish: but
he That keepeth the law, happy is he.

Proverbs 29: 18

The consequence of lack of vision takes a progressive decline to an end point. Where there is no vision, the journey to a sad end commences. The fact that people perish for lack of vision is the ultimate end of the journey. In between, there are many consequences that a life without vision suffers. Living with or without a vision is a journey. Either may take the same length of time but one thing is certain, their destinations differ. The sad end of a life without vision does not respect colour, creed or class of men. Where there is no vision, the people any people of any nation, colour, race or tribe stand the risk of perishing. The result cuts across all people, irrespective of geographical locations or family backgrounds.

WHAT IS VISION?

Vision is the power to stand out from the crowd. It is the distinguishing identity of a man. Men of vision don't belong to the rank and file of humanity. They stand out!

Vision is the power that motivates a man to do the impossible thing. It is the drive to achieve an incredible feat. Men of vision flex their muscles where men without vision chicken out. Your attitude to life reveals your vision or lack of it!

Proverbs 29:18 reveals the ultimate result for lack of vision. Many people don't see it this way. It is only by spending time to meditate on it that this truth jumps out. What it means to perish is, to waste away, expire, get destroyed, become desolate or ruined. Each of those words connotes strong negative sense. We can therefore say that lack of vision puts one on the negative side of life.

Looking at some Biblical examples, we have an idea of the general consequences of lack of vision before such people eventually perished. Their cases make it obvious that living without a vision is the worst evil anyone can ever do to himself. The enemy would gladly capitalize on that to inflict more injuries to such lives. The way of recovery from the power of the enemy is, first and foremost, to find our vision in life.

In Israel, vision in the days before Samuel was born was very scarce and private. Vision here means divine revelations channelled to a people through a prophet.

A prophet is otherwise known as a seer in the Old Testament.

> *"Beforetime in Israel, when a man went to enquire of God, thus he spake, Come, and let us go to the seer: for he that is now called a Prophet was beforetime called a seer."*
> **1Samuel 9:9**

The way of recovery from the power of the enemy is, first and foremost, to find our Vision in life.

Any genuine vision therefore has its origin in

7

God. Men of vision see something that others don't. In this sense, every man or woman of vision is a seer! There is something they see that others don't. Abraham looked at the stars in heaven and *saw* his future glorious children. He looked again at the sand on the seashore and *saw* his uncountable posterity. In both cases, other men around him might have looked at the stars and the sand to see nothing more than the geographical beauty of the earth. Abraham saw what he did because God was in it. In the days when God raised Samuel as a prophet, many things were wrong in the land for nothing else but lack of vision. Let us check part of the account in the Bible.

And the child Samuel ministered unto the LORD before Eli. And the word of the LORD was precious in those days; there was no open vision. And all Israel from Dan even to Beersheba knew that Samuel was established to be a prophet of the LORD.

1 Samuel 3: 1, 20

The word of the Lord, the vehicle for divine vision, was very scarce in those days. In the entire land, there was no man with audacity of vision to whom the nation could make recourse in time of national need. There were a few but irregular occasions of visions among a few persons though, but their level of vision was not enough to salvage or pilot the destiny of the nation.

A man is as important as the size of his vision. Samuel's plunge into open vision stood him out as someone the nation could depend upon for guidance and direction in national affairs. The audacity of his open visions instantly stood him out in the land. On account of his vision, he effortlessly won national honour and fame. The level of honour and fame a man enjoys is a function of the size of his vision. His example teaches us to think and dream real big.

Since genuine visions have their origin in God, they are usually bigger than men! We should not let human reasoning hinder or trim down the size of vision the Lord is willing to give us. He impacts visions and provides the enablement to perform them.

MORAL DECLINE AND CONTEMPT

What happened before Samuel began to declare divine visions in the land? There was general moral decline. There was general lack of respect for God's service, moral decline is a proof of lack of vision. A man of vision keeps high moral integrity. Joseph kept his moral integrity because his eyes were fixed on his vision. During the time of Samuel, the land had grown stinking with moral decline and the place of worship had become badly affected. The Bible says:

> "Now the sons of Eli were sons of Belial; they knew not the LORD. And the priests' custom with the people was, that, when any man offered sacrifice, the priest's servant came, while the flesh was in seething, with a flesh hook of three teeth in his hand; And he struck it into the pan, or kettle, or caldron, or pot; all that the flesh hook brought up the priest took for himself. So they did in Shiloh unto all the Israelites that came thither. Also before they burnt the fat, the priest's servant came, and said to the man that sacrificed, Give flesh to roast for the priest; for he will not have sodden flesh of thee, but raw. And if any man said unto him,

Let them not fail to burn the fat presently, and then take as much as thy soul desireth; then he would answer him, Nay; but thou shalt give it me now: and if not, I will take it by force. Wherefore the sin of the young men was very great before the LORD: for men abhorred the offering of the LORD.

1 Samuel 2: 12-17

Vision affects our morality. Morality is ethics, integrity, uprightness, principle and decency. Everything in life is guided by some principles. In places of worship, in business, in academic activities, just in any area of human endeavour, principles run through everything we do. A man without vision despises the principles for success in any chosen field. He becomes a failure anywhere you put him. This is why people without vision fail in ministry, business, marriage and career or anywhere they are found. Their failure simply results from lack of vision, that is, lack of understanding and adherence to the principles of success required in a particular field. Eli's sons were the priests in the days of Samuel. Their carefree attitude to divine service clearly contravened the principles guiding the operations of their office. They lacked vision of their call; therefore, they grossly violated the ethics of the irreligious profession. There are ethics in every profession, lack of vision on career prospects and development in any chosen profession is one of the reasons these ethics are violated. It is a grave tragedy of life when men entrusted with noble positions compromise for lack of vision.

Their bad example spreads faster than wild fire. Their ill-fated example badly influences others, and the precedence for future compromise of morals is laid for posterity. We often hear people say that Africa's only natural disaster is bad leadership. How true! Just pick any African country as a case study and you will be amazed by the negative influence of bad leadership on people's attitude, the economy, politics and general way of life. Bad leadership is a product of leadership without vision. Eli's sons were spiritual leaders but their leadership example only made the people to develop contempt for the services of God. Concerning them, the Bible says:

'Wherefore the sin of the young men was very great before the LORD: for men abhorred the offering of the LORD'

1 Samuel 2: 17.

Compromise and contempt characterise a life without vision. Lack of vision defeats purpose in the lives of those who attend church services. You don't come to church to show off your dress, shoes or class. You come to church to find God. You are in the church to find God and you have to be desperate to find Him. God is not coming for those who are full. If you are already filled up, there is no place for Him to fill. God is coming to fill the empty souls and to give life to those who lack it. Finding purpose for whatever you do is vision.

A young man was asked to cite the portion of the Bible he likes best and he said: 'I like the New Testament. It is my best. 'He was asked again:' In what book of the New Testament is your favourite portion?'He answered: 'The book of parables. 'Of course, everyone knows that there is no book of Parables in the Bible. The young man

13

simply lacked understanding of the word. He comes to church but doesn't know anything about purpose in church attendance. His lack of vision makes him an ignorant person. It costs more to be ignorant than to have knowledge. Ignorance is the worst state any man can be in. In its final stage, ignorance causes men to perish as we learnt that

"My people are destroyed for lack of knowledge:..."

Hosea 4: 6.

A man is as important as the size of his dream.

The founding fathers of United States of America were full of vision that transcended their generation. It was visionary of them to have laid the foundation of that great country on the God of all nations. The same is true of the United Kingdom which once produced great minds like King James who piloted the translation of the Bible into English. The efforts of visionary leaders and individuals in these countries, as well as in other countries of the world, sharply contrast the growing level of moral decline and contempt for hallowed institutions like marriage, governance and schools in today's world. We can look at our age and say where there is no vision, lawlessness abounds.

LACK OF DIRECTION

Where there is no vision, there is lack of direction, focus and result. We find another Biblical case study in **Amos 8: 11-12** which states:

> *"Behold, the days come, saith the Lord GOD, that I will send a famine in the land, not a famine of bread, nor a thirst for water, but of hearing the words of the LORD: And they shall wander from sea to sea, and from the north even to the east, they shall run to and fro to seek the word of the LORD, and shall not find it."*

Through Amos, God forewarned the people of an impending famine not food famine but the famine of divine revelation. In one word, there was going to be famine of visions! Amos went on to give the graphic and gory consequences of life without vision. From his account, we can infer

15

that a life without vision has the following features: Wandering aimlessly and running in vain; these two words wandering and running were directly used by Amos. Pause for a while and think on them and see how they affect or describe your life. Doing this will help you recover yourself from lack of vision or help consolidate your effort at the pursuit of your vision. People without vision wander about aimlessly. They have no goal, no pursuit and no direction. They depend on chance and luck. They are at the mercy of the circumstances of life. They are always drifting from place to place; from one organization to another and sometimes, they drift from church to church. Although change is important to achieving any set goal in life, the frequency of change wanderers make only shows that they lack vision. Geographically, Israel was to wander from the Mediterranean to the Dead Sea and from the North to the South during the famine of vision which Amos foretold. It is not enough to relocate from one geographical location to another except there location is occasioned by vision. Traversing land and seas in search of nothing will achieve nothing. Travelling abroad or from one end of the world to another without vision is a waste of time and resources. Vision gives direction to the traveller. We can look at the life of Abraham and David and say they wandered at some point in time. They did! You find them always relocating from place to place. What makes their case totally different is that their relocation was divinely motivated. It is the involvement of God in our journey that imparts vision for our mission. The Bible tells us that

"...in thy light shall we see light."
Psalm 36: 9.

The light of God's instruction, direction or mandate gives us light in our path. That light is the vision we need to travel. It defines our path and distinguishes it from others.' A man or woman of vision does not copy anybody. He or she is very original in his or her own right. There is something fresh and new in every vision God imparts to men. You need not copy anybody if you have a vision for living. In marriage, you will wander from sister to sister or from brother to brother if you lack vision of a life partner. You

17

can keep changing jobs or departments in your organization if you lack vision. You will still lack fulfilment when you don't have vision. Vision stabilizes a man. It fixes your focus on a goal and directs your energy towards it. Daniel made it very plain that where vision is sealed, concealed or hidden from men, they run to and fro. His words picture a state of confusion when there is no vision. Anxiety, aimless effort and profitless competition result from lack of vision. He said:

> *"But thou, O Daniel, shut up the words, and seal the book, even to the time of the end: many shall run to and fro, and knowledge shall be increased.*
>
> **Daniel 12: 4**

A careful study of the lives of the children of Israel under the Old Testament would make us to develop a sense of appreciation for men of vision, teaching us to be visionary in our generation. Each time there was no priest to teach the Law and no prophet to make exposition of divine truth or provide guidance, you find the people idle, exposed and deviant as explained below:

1.   Idle They were idle in the sense that they lacked direction on how and what to expend their human and natural resources. You cannot have a vision and stay idle. Vision fuels the energy for achievement. The first thing I suspect in any idle life is lack of vision.

2.   Exposed Lack of vision exposes man to danger and confusion. If you can't think for yourself, others will think for you; often, to your disadvantage. You need vision to personally take charge; otherwise, you may forever remain a follower when you should be a leader.

3.   Deviant Lack of vision promoted deviant behaviour in the children of Israel. They rebelled against God and against constituted authority. A case in mind was when they lost vision of Canaan and evolved the golden calf in the wilderness. They rebelled against God, the giver of the vision; and against Moses, the agent of communication of the Vision. You will find more on the channels of communicating vision in the latter part of this book. Their deviant behaviour made them to consider returning to Egypt, the house of

19

bondage. Where there is no vision, for a people to perish is the final end in a chain of its consequences. Many of today's global problems bother on lack of vision. A genuine vision does not only come from God, its impact reaches to generations unborn. If your vision does not outlive you, your pursuit is greatly limited. The beauty of any vision is to continue even after the demise of the visionary.

We still have the Methodists today because of the vision of John Wesley assisted by his brother Charles. The Baptist cannot forget Charles Haddon Spurgeon. Beneficiaries of the Reformers' labour cannot forget Lutheran effort till today. These were men of vision who lived and passed on their vision to others. Continuity is a test of true vision. How far into the future does your vision extend?

A man without vision despises the principles for success in any chosen field. He becomes a failure anywhere you put him.

Where there is no vision,
there is lack of direction,
focus and result.

Travelling abroad or from one end
of the world to another without vision is
a waste of time and resources.
Vision gives direction to the traveller.

2 Vision Makes A Leader

'Vision is the ability to get people to do what they don't want to do in order to achieve what they want to achieve in life.' - **Tom Landry**

Vision is one of the greatest requirements for leadership. If your résumé does not describe you as a visionary person, aiming for any leadership position in the church or in secular organizations is unnecessary. Vision makes a leader; a good and true leader for that matter. Leadership trainings, seminars and literature always emphasize educational acquisition, communication skills development, ability to listen to suggestions, control over temperament, developing a team spirit, to mention but a few, among other qualities a good leader should possess. One weakness I have found about this list is that vision is often omitted.

23

To me, good leadership begins with being visionary; every other thing should follow. Take vision away from a leader, he becomes worse than the worst follower. A leader does not only know the way; he shows the way and walks the way. In his light, the path of his followers is lit and they confidently take their journey, even to a most unfamiliar terrain, trusting in nothing but the vision of their leader. Landry's view of vision introduces another dimension to it. He sees vision as the ability to recognize and utilize human resources for common good. This view differentiates leaders from followers.

A leader sees potentials in his followers and taps into them in the interest of all.

> **Take vision away from a leader, he becomes worse than the worst follower. A leader does not only know the way;**
> **he shows the way and walks the way.**

Tom Landry (1924-2000) was an American player and coach. He was rated as one of the most successful coaches in the history of National

Football League (NFL). As a coach, he was a leader over his team; so his idea on visionary leadership is partly from the success of his personal experience. Recognizing and utilizing the resources of the team he trained was an essential factor in his success story.

Expanding his angle to vision and leadership, we can draw two points as stated below:

A visionary leader is insightful
A visionary leader is a trainer

These two outstanding qualities of a visionary leader were clearly demonstrated in the life and ministry of Christ, the greatest Leader that ever lived. He looked at Peter and from the insight He gained into the future usefulness of a then Lilly-livered follower, He said to him:

> *"And he brought him to Jesus. And When Jesus beheld him, he said, Thou art Simon the son of Jonah: thou shalt be called Cephas, which is by interpretation, A stone".*
>
> **John 1: 42**

25

THE POWER OF INSIGHT

The insight of a visionary leader helps him to look beyond immediate cloud of problems to the solution ahead. It is this vision that helps such leaders to forge ahead in their pursuit where others fizzle out. A visionary leader is driven by his vision while a leader without vision is driven by circumstances. Jesus fixed his gaze on Peter for a while and saw strength in his weakness. That penetrative gaze enabled Christ to gain insight into the person of Peter. In this zealous and restless follower, He saw a mixture of strength and weakness. Christ knew the danger this mixture portends in any life. He shifted emphasis to the foreseen strength of Peter and branded him Mr. Stone.

A visionary leader does not concentrate attention on problems. He does not pretend as if problems are not real though, he rather concentrates efforts on finding solution to problems. From being called Peter to being called Cephas, that is, Stone; Jesus repositioned the mind of Peter to have a positive view of himself. One of the greatest limitations ever imposed on any man is from the way the man perceives himself.

Gideon perceived himself as belonging to an unfortunate generation where God's benevolence was scarce. He perceived himself as unlucky to have come from an unpopular background in Israel. As he went on to spin out more factors against his success in life, the Lord interrupted him and we are told:

> *"And the LORD looked upon him, and said, Go in this thy might, and thou shalt save Israel from the hand of the Midianites: have not I sent thee?"*
> **Judges 6: 14**

A visionary leader helps people to discover their worth, talents and potentials. He sees in them what they don't even see in themselves. Leadership that is committed to bringing out the best in you is visionary. Such leaders make impact to the political or economical development of a nation because they can perceive the human and natural resources at their disposal. America has won the name *'land of opportunities'* over several decades because the leadership of this great nation is committed to providing opportunity for self-actualization. It works arduously, through legislations, reviews of existing laws and policies, tore move all barriers to utmost fulfilment in individual and corporate lives of the Americans. Doing this is nothing short of being visionary. To the credit of its visionary leaders, America's foreign nationals and immigrants from all walks of live, alongside their American citizens counterparts, have won the country laurels in all fields of life.

The insight of a visionary leader helps him to look beyond immediate clouds of problems to the solution Horizon ahead.

Albert Einstein (1879-1955), was a German-born American Physicist and Nobel Laureate. He is best known as the creator of the special and general theories of relativity and for his bold hypothesis concerning the particle of nature of light. He is still considered the most well-known scientist of the 20th century and one of the greatest minds of all times.

Einstein was a genius with incredible weakness.

We leant that he was known to suffer from dyslexia because of his bad memory and his constant failure to memorize the simplest things. Some writers also said he sometimes would not remember the months in the year yet he would solve some of the most complicated mathematical formulas of the time without any trouble.

The great mathematician and physicist did not speak until he was three years of age. Most parents would have written off a child like that without knowing that beneath the temporary disability was a permanent ability. He had a tough time learning mathematics in school, later to become a world class mathematician. Einstein also found it hard to express himself in writing, yet he grew through all these to register his name in the hall of fame. There are men like Einstein today, your seeming impediment today can be turned into a gold mine if you can have a functional vision in your life. You cannot be stopped by the many challenges there are in your life if only you can have vision. While others concentrate on their weaknesses, a visionary leader looks at the beauty of their potentials. To a visionary leader, something good can still come out of Nazareth. Your vision about yourself will help you to overcome any barrier you may encounter along the way. Vision is a propeller!

A visionary leader does not run down people and make them feel they are good for nothing. He sees something good in every bad situation or person. Vision is the insight he gains into such situations and persons. As a leader, what good thing have you seen in your followers or subordinates? If you can't point to any one yet, you may have lost the power of vision. Stop, think and re-launch yourself.

Without vision, a potentially profitable business, through rebranding, would be thrown away.

THE IMPORTANCE OF REBRANDING
In modern world, what Jesus did to Peter is called rebranding. Without vision, a potentially profitable business, would be thrown away. You can turn any situation around through rebranding

and get the best out of it. The Encarta English Dictionary defines branding as a name, usually a trademark, of a product or manufacturer, or the product identified by this name. Rebranding is therefore, re-naming, reconstructing a trade mark or changing identity of something or somebody. God started the business of branding and rebranding. He re-packaged Abram to Abraham, associating the new, brand name with *'father of many nations'* as a catchphrase or tag line.

Each time the name Abraham was called, the old man had a different picture of himself. From a childless old man, he saw a father of many nations in himself. A visionary leader gets people aligned with his vision. Until they see what you have seen, they can never become part of your pursuit! Elisha was unruffled when he saw the army of Syria surging towards him to arrest and extradite him. He had seen the vision of the superior but invisible army of heaven positioned all over the mountains and plains around him. In number, the invisible army was more and in strength, the Syrian army was no match. His vision of the reinforcement from heaven made him calm but

Gehazi, his servant, was terribly afraid because he was yet to receive Elisha's vision. Elisha did what every visionary leader should do. He prayed for Gehazi to see what he had seen. A part from teaching, preaching and instructing men on your vision, you have to pray for God to enable them see what vision He has given you. Elisha's account with his servant reads:

> *"And when the servant of the man of God was risen early, and gone forth, behold, an host compassed the city both with horses and chariots. And his servant said unto him, Alas, my master! How shall we do? And he answered, Fear not: for they that be with us are more than they that be with them. And Elisha prayed, and said, LORD, I pray thee, open his eyes, that he may see. And the LORD opened the eyes of the young man; and he saw: and, behold, the mountain was full of horses and chariots of fire roundabout Elisha."* **2 Kings 6: 15-17**

Your followers must see what you have seen to give you the support you deserve. If they have a different picture in their minds, rebrand them by changing the image on their minds with the blueprint of your vision. That way, they will be unruffled in the face of any challenge just as you are. They must see what you see to follow what you follow! Branding is important to achieving attitudinal change. People's attitude changes in response to branding or rebranding.

Many products and services once rejected are now accepted simply because they are rebranded. It is the insight of a visionary leader that makes him see the need to rebrand a product, service or people for a set goal. From seeing himself as weakling in character, Peter was rebranded to have a different and positive view of himself. He was born with a character flaw as anyone else, but God saw something else in him. He was given a new picture of himself to help him align with how God sees him. A visionary leader has a benchmark, a blue print towards which his activities are directed.

One of the greatest limitations ever imposed on any man is from the way The man perceives himself.

THE PLACE OF TRAINING

David was an insightful leader. He was also a perfect trainer. I am going to give you an instance in his life that shows his outstanding ability at successfully training the most unlikely candidates for success. He was driven by his vision for victory over his enemies to undertake training for the worst class of men. We are told:

> *"David therefore departed thence, and escaped to the cave Adullam: and when his brethren and all his father's house heard it, they went down thither to him. And every one that was in distress, and every one that was in debt, and every one that was discontented, gathered themselves unto him; and he became a captain over them: and there were with him about four hundred men."*
>
> **1 Samuel 22: 1-2**

David had a very terrible congregation to manage at this point in his life. The social qualities of these people would put any pastor off. In his flight from Saul and his conspirators, David had to assume leadership position over a people described as:

Distressed
Indebted
Discontented
Limited in population strength

This is not a congregation from which a pastor should expect fat envelops of tithes and offerings. The people were in need themselves because they were in debts. Certainly, this kind of congregation cannot support the personal life and ministry of the pastor. The people here cannot contribute to missionary assignment of the minister.

They probably needed more financial help than their pastor! Not only this. Members of this congregation could not make David, their pastor, happy because they were distressed and discontented. They could not lift the spirit of their pastor because their own spirits were down. Their population strength of 400men was a disadvantage to David's plight when considered against the army of enemies that had gathered behind Saul against him. Does the above picture describe your situation as a pastor, missionary or minister of the gospel? Does it describe your circumstance as a leader? What is your assessment of the people under your leadership? Is there anything to be done in a situation like this? Let us go back to the example of David and find out what he did. David began to train and re-orientate the people for better use. This is the first assignment of a visionary leader to change people's orientation or perspective about life and about themselves. Later on, when David was divinely advised to help the men of Keilah against the Philistine's invasion, he went to the battle with 600 soldiers. Some of these must have been drawn and trained from the original population of indebted, discontented and distressed people he had to manage.

A visionary leader sees every man and woman, and everything around him as raw materials capable of being converted to fulfilling his vision. It takes vision to see opportunities in problems. The problem of fatal persecution the Jerusalem church suffered became an opportunity for the indiscriminate spread of the gospel. In the light of your vision, every problem is an advantage! Abraham was a visionary leader and a trainer as well. During his nomadic life, he made out time to train the servants born in his house. He later employed them as soldiers to rescue Lot, his cousin, from the captivity of confederate kings who invaded Lot's territory.

"And it came to pass in the days of Amraphel king of Shinar, Arioch king of Ellasar, Chedorlaomer king of Elam, and Tidal king of nations; That these made war with Bera king of Sodom, and with Birsha king of Gomorrah, Shinab king of Admah, and Shemeber king of Zeboiim, and the king of Bela, which is Zoar. And they took Lot, Abram's brother's son, who dwelt in Sodom, and his goods, and departed. And there came one that had escaped, and told Abram the Hebrew; for he dwelt in the plain of Mamre the Amorite, brother of Eshcol, and brother of Aner: and these were confederate with Abram. And when Abram heard that his brother was taken captive, he armed his trained servants, born in his own house, three hundred and eighteen, and pursued them unto Dan.
And he divided himself against them, he and his servants, by night, and smote them, and pursued

them unto Hobah, which is on the left hand of Damascus. And he brought back all the goods, and also brought again his brother Lot, and his goods, and the women also, and the people.

Genesis 14: 1-2, 12-16

A visionary leader does not look for a ready made people to inherit and pastor. His vision drives him to training the people available to him no matter how raw they are. Jesus trained His disciples for three and half years. He conducted the training through:

Direct teaching

His practical examples

Field work

Any responsible leadership would not downplay the importance of training and re-training of his followers or subordinates. Training brings out the best in people. It better equips them for future services. It takes being visionary to expose people to seminars, retreats and other platforms of training in order to bring out the best in them.

It takes being visionary to expose people to seminars, retreats and other platforms of training in order to Bring out the best in them.

Elizabeth 1 (1533-1603), queen of England and Ireland (1558-1603), was the longest reigning English monarch in about two centuries. She was also the first woman to successfully occupy the English throne. Her history depicts her as a visionary leader. She understood the importance of managing human resources in the interest of future development of the nation.

Mark Kishlansky, A.B, A.M, PhD and Baird Professor of history, Harvard University in an article about the Elizabethan period wrote that: "The difficulties Elizabeth experienced governing the English state were enhanced by prejudices against women rulers. Though she presented herself in the traditional images of the monarchy, such as carrying the sword of state, commissioning a portrait showing her bestriding the counties of England, and even appearing in armour, Elizabeth realized the importance of

39

securing the cooperation of powerful men in order to rule effectively. She made extensive use of the Privy Council and summoned ten parliaments during her reign.

The 45-year reign of Elizabeth I as queen of England and Ireland (1558-1603) was so influential it became known as the Elizabethan Age. During her rule, Elizabeth helped shaped the future of England, creating a stable monarchy, developing legal institutions, encouraging commerce, establishing the Protestant religion as England's faith, and defending the nation against Spanish forces.

In 1601, near the end of her reign, Elizabeth delivered to Parliament what came to be known as her Golden Speech. The speech demonstrates Elizabeth's skills of oratory as well as her devotion to her people. The speech delivered on November 1601 is contained in *The Penguin Book of Historic Speeches,* MacArthur, Brian, ed. Penguin Books, 1996."

The Queen's ability at recognizing and utilizing the human resources in her time stands her out as one of the most visionary leaders of any age. There is always a price to pay to make your vision a reality. In business, there is a price to pay in order to profit. The road up is not an easy one but it costs more to be down.

Any man without vision does not command or lead people. Instead of leading, he is led. Vision makes a leader. When people buy into your vision, they will leave everything else to follow you. Vision commands followership.

The power of vision motivates. As the mountaineer weathers the storms to reach the highest summit in life, so a man of vision surges through all odds to reach his goal. Vision provides the motivation for achievement. You can only go as far as your vision in life.

3 Vision Consumes

"A shared vision is not an idea. It is not even an important idea such as freedom. It is, rather, a force in people's hearts, a force of impressive power...shared vision is vital for the learning organization because it provides the focus and energy for learning." - **Peter M. Senge**, U.S. Business Executive and author.

As fire consumes a forest so vision consumes the soul with unstoppable passion and energy. Peter Senge's use of the word 'force' to describe the power of vision makes it further clearer that vision is not passive but active in the life of the visionary. As a force in the heart, Senge explains that vision provides focus and energy for learning. The force of vision consumes the visionary with motion. Force produces motion according to scientists and from everyday, common sense experience. Push a stationary bucket, for instance, it will move in proportion to the force you apply. You can never remain static with a genuine vision in your heart. The force of your vision must keep you moving in the direction of its objective. In physics, force is considered any action or influence that accelerates an object or that causes motion. Physicists say force is a vector quantity which has direction and magnitude.

What this means is that any force can be measured to determine its value or size otherwise known as its magnitude. And each time a force is applied, it has a specific direction it follows. Vision as a force in the heart also has magnitude and direction. These unique qualities of the force of vision differentiate it from other kinds of motivations. How do you know the value or size of a force applied to an object without measuring it with scientific instruments? We can have a rough idea of it by looking at the impact of the force against the size of the object. A big force is required to move a big object, just as a small force is required to move a small object. The amount of force required to push a car is far less than the amount of force required to push a heavy truck. Therefore, the magnitude of your vision can be measured by its impact in real life. A small vision pursues small things and a big vision runs after big things. On the issue of direction as the second quality of force in relation to vision, the specific goal or objective of a vision is its direction. A true vision from God provides direction.

A man of vision is never confused about what to do and where to go. The force of his vision provides motion and direction for him. I am yet to see a man of vision static in life. Vision produces motion because it is a force in the heart of man. Sometimes, the man just discovers to his amazement that something keeps him moving in spite of all odds. That is the force of vision; it consumes like fire! The disciples of Jesus represent a life truly set ablaze by vision. The power of their vision to preach the gospel motivated these largely unrefined disciples to face and overcome the worst oppositions of their time. They were unstoppable; they could not be silenced and their impact could not be denied.

45

"Then the high priest rose up, and all they that were with him, (which is the sect of the Sadducees,) and were filled with indignation, And laid their hands on the apostles, and put them in the common prison.

But the angel of the Lord by night opened the prison doors, and brought them forth, and said ,Go, stand and speak in the temple to the people all the words of this life. And when they heard that, they entered into the temple early in the morning, and taught. But the high priest came, and they that were with him, and called the council together, and all the senate of the children of Israel, and sent to the prison to have them brought. But when the officers came, and found them not in the prison, they returned, and told, Saying, The prison truly found we shut with all safety, and the keepers standing without before the doors: but when we had opened, we found no man within. Now when the high priest and the captain of the temple and the chief priests heard these things, they doubted of them whereunto this would grow.

Then came one and told them, saying, Behold, the men whom ye put in prison are standing in the temple, and teaching the people. Then went the captain with the officers, and brought them without violence: for they feared the people, lest they should have been stoned. And when they had brought them, they set them before the council: and the high priest asked them, Saying, Did not we straitly command you that ye should not teach in this name? and, behold, ye have filled Jerusalem with your doctrine, and intend to bring this man's blood upon us.

Then Peter and the other apostles answered and said, We ought to obey God rather than men."

Acts5: 17-29

It is a spiritual principle that the greater your anointing; the stronger and more in number the forces of opposition to face.

Men and women consumed with their visions have a singular purpose. I recall a short story about a king whose servant had to help get medicine. Titled 'Put Your Mind To What You Are Doing,'
the story reads:

"This Eastern legend is about a king who was sick. He sent one of his servants to go across the town and bring him a bowl of previous medicine from the Chemist's store. The trade fair that was going on made it difficult to safeguard the liquid. However, he did so without spilling one drop. 'How is it that you could bring the potion so quickly without spilling any when the streets were so crowded?' The king asked. And the servant simply answered 'I was thinking only of the medicine. I noticed nothing but the bowl in my hands.'"

When you are consumed with your vision, you will be able to avoid the distractions on the way to your destiny fulfilment. There are detours along the way; and there are detractors who pretend as co-workers. The power of focus derived from the force of your vision is the only way to overcome them. In the strength of their vision, the disciples withstood threats to their lives, legislation opposed to freedom of assembly, laws contrary to freedom of religious affiliation and worship and imprisonment without trial. The flames of their burning vision empowered them to go through all these and in defiance to their circumstances, they confidently said:

"...We ought to obey God rather than men..."

The consuming fire of vision provokes loyalty in two directions:
§ Loyalty to the source of the vision God
§ Loyalty to the terms of the vision

The Apostles expressed their loyalty to God when they bluntly told the Pharisees and the Sadducees "We would rather obey God than men." They also expressed their loyalty to the terms of their vision when, upon being delivered from prison through angelic intervention, they were found

"standing in the temple, and teaching the people."

The consuming flames of your vision must produce loyalty to God. Moses was rated as faithful or loyal to God in all things pertaining to the service of the Lord. David too was found faithful to God in his generation. In both cases, the loyalty of these men found expression in their attitude to the services of God. Paul, the apostle, revealed part of the secrets behind his outstanding success in ministry work. Immediately he got God's call to preach the gospel to the Gentiles, he said

"But when it pleased God who separated me from my mother's womb, and called me by his grace, to reveal his Son in me, that I might preach him among the heathen; immediately I conferred not with flesh and blood."

Galatians 1:5-6

He held no conference with men on whether to obey God or not. He was not ready to take any piece of advice contrary to the divine instruction he had received. Above that, he was not ready to comply with the dictates of his own flesh to abandon God's mandate upon his life. That is what is called faithfulness or loyalty to God. On the loyalty to the terms of his vision, he knew the world of the world of the Gentiles was his parish and wasted no time in exploring the unreached territory of the Gentile nations. His message was very consistent "Jesus Christ, and Him crucified..."

That was his passion; his message and his pursuit. It was the summary of his vision.

When your vision consumes you, it gets you out of normalcy to a bit of abnormality. People will just notice something they think is out of place about you. It is normal to be abnormal when vision consumes the heart.

NEHEMIAH BUILDS FROM RUBBLES

Nehemiah had a vision to rebuild the broken walls of Jerusalem and restore the dignity of divine worship in the land. His vision was communicated to him as a burden in his heart consequent on the information he heard about the plight of the people in Jerusalem. The account was recorded thus:

"The words of Nehemiah the son of Hachaliah. And it came to pass in the month Chisleu, in the twentieth year, as I was in Shushan the palace, That Hanani, one of my brethren, came, he and certain men of Judah; and I asked them

concerning the Jews that had escaped, which were left of the captivity, and concerning Jerusalem. And they said unto me, The remnant that are left of the captivity there in the province are in great affliction and reproach: the wall of Jerusalem also is broken down, and the gates thereof are burned with fire. And it came to pass, when I heard these words, that I sat down and wept, and mourned certain days, and fasted, and prayed before the God of heaven."

Nehemiah 1: 1-4

We all receive our visions in various forms and ways, under different circumstances, times and places. All true visions have their origin in God. The information Nehemiah heard about his people in Jerusalem took his sleep off him, sent him praying and fasting and got him heavy in the heart. The inner condition of this man soon showed on his facial appearance and it was not too long when his boss noticed that something was wrong with him. When your vision consumes you, it gets you out of normalcy to a bit of abnormality. People will just notice something they think is out of place about you. It is normal to be abnormal when vision consumes the heart. The burden was so much in Nehemiah's heart that he sought permission for leave of absence for days longer than his work schedule required. As a Personal Assistant to a foreign president, it was not normal to apply for a leave of absence for the length of time his took.

A man driven by vision cannot do everything normally anymore. Your vision would make you take steps the world would consider foolish. To them, it is abnormal but it is normal for a man of vision. To the world, it was not normal for Pastor E. A. Adeboye to drop the ambition of becoming the youngest Vice Chancellor in Africa to pick up the microphone for gospel preaching. But in pursuit of his vision, it was a very normal thing to do. The committee of persecutors in Jerusalem that had Paul as its henchman found it absurd and totally abnormal to hear that he had decamped to the same faith he was authorized and commissioned to persecute.

In the agenda of God for Paul, to defend the gospel he was sent to destroy was normal but abnormal for the Pharisees and the Sadducees. In pursuit of his vision, Nehemiah had two classes of detractors to overcome:

The first class were enemies that conspired against the work. They were territorial or environmental forces whose names were given as Sanballat, Tobiah, Arabians, the Ammonites and the Ashdodites. You must know the environmental or territorial forces against you in your location if you want to succeed with your vision. The Bible says:

> *"But it came to pass, that when Sanballat heard that we builded the wall, he was wroth, and took great indignation, and mocked the Jews. And he spake before his brethren and the army of Samaria, and said, What do these feeble Jews? will they fortify themselves? Will they sacrifice? will they make an end in a day? Will they revive the stones out of the heaps of the rubbish which are burned? Now Tobiah the Ammonite was by him, and he said, Even that which they build, if a fox go up, he shall even break down their stonewall. Hear, O our God; for we are despised: and turn their reproach upon their own head, and*

give them for a prey in the land of captivity: And cover not their iniquity, and let not their sin be blotted out from before thee: for they have provoked thee to anger before the builders.

So built we the wall; and all the wall was joined together unto the half thereof: for the people had a mind to work. But it came to pass, that when Sanballat, and Tobiah, and the Arabians, and the Ammonites, and the Ashdodites, heard that the walls of Jerusalem were made up, and that the breaches began to be stopped, then they were very wroth, And conspired all of them together to come and to fight against Jerusalem, and to hinder it. Nevertheless we made our prayer unto our God, and set a watch against them day and night, because of them."

Nehemiah 4:1-9

These external forces ganged up against the progress of the work and fought to stop the vision. There is no vision without an enemy. In fact, that it is a vision from God makes it liable to the attacks of the enemies. The degree of attacks suffered often varies with the importance and scope of a man's vision. For this reason, a man with a vision to do what none else has ever done should be prepared to suffer what none else has ever suffered. How much the devil troubles you over your vision shows the importance attached to the vision you carry. People had been praying and obtaining answers to prayers before and during the time of Daniel. But when he began to pray in line with the vision to liberate Israel from the 70-year Babylonian captivity, the prince of Persia withstood answer to that prayer for 21 days. One way to derive courage to forge ahead in the pursuit of your vision is to relate the significance of your vision to the difficulties you are going through. You may not fully know, but the devil knows the full importance of your vision in the agenda of God for mankind.

It is a spiritual principle that the greater your anointing; the stronger and more in number the forces of opposition to face. Elijah was to be arrested by a captain of fifty and his fifty soldiers. Twice, he botched the attempted arrest by commanding fire upon them. For Elisha who got twice of the power of Elijah, a whole army of Syria was dispatched to arrest him. Of course, he too commanded spiritual blindness upon them such that they did not know he was the man declared wanted. Similarly, a great vision calls for great opposition and attacks. Don't be discouraged; your vision maybe far more important than you are looking at it. Unfortunately, the devil knows what you may not know about your vision. If not, why do you think he has to bother himself so much with what you are doing?

The second class of enemies you must prepare to meet in pursuit of your vision are internal forces or enemies within. These may represent some members of your congregation or ministry. In extended case, they also represent household or local wickedness. Their job may be to discourage those supporting your vision even when they have nothing to offer to support it themselves. A look at how Nehemiah handled them will be found helpful.

"And Judah said, The strength of the bearers of burdens is decayed, and there is much rubbish; so that we are not able to build the wall.

And our adversaries said, They shall not know, neither see, till we come in the midst among them, and slay them, and cause the work to cease.

And it came to pass, that when the Jews which dwelt by them came, they said unto us ten times, from all places whence ye shall return unto us they will be upon you. Therefore set I in the lower places behind the wall, and on the higher places, I even set the people after their families with their swords, their spears, and their bows."

Nehemiah 4: 10-13

Nehemiah tackled these two classes of enemies with prayer and vigilance. When the flames of vision consume our souls, releasing unstoppable energies for accomplishment, maintaining a corresponding prayer life and watchfulness against the enemies' antics is a necessity. The confessions of the following men, some of which I have paraphrased, provide an insight into the power of a consuming vision:

"Oh, that I may burn out for Christ" **Henry Martin**

"I am ready to die in Jerusalem for Christ's sake"
Paul the Apostle

"The whole world is my parish" **John Wesley**

"Give me Scotland or I die." **John Knox**

"If I perish, I perish."- **Queen Esther**

"God has commanded me to move mountains; I have no business with pebbles"- **Reinhard Bonke**

"If I have only one jacket left, I am ready to give it up in defence of the gospel" **W.F Kumuyi**

"A discovery of vision and its pursuits is the gateway to the actualization of our glorious destiny in Christ."
David. O Oyedepo

"Pressure is God's tool for extracting gold from dross. Are you pressurized because of Jesus? Congrats! Your gold is coming..."- **E.A Adeboye**

Your life will no more be important except in fulfilling that singular goal of your vision!

Your vision would make you take steps the world would consider foolish. To them, it is abnormal but it is normal for a man of vision.

Vision is not passive but active in the life of the visionary.

Therefore, the magnitude of your vision can be measured by its impact in real life. A small vision pursues small things and a big vision runs after big things.

4 Vision Dares!

All serious daring starts from within.

A man of vision is daring! Your vision will make you dare to be different from others in your generation, family background and environment. The Wright brothers dared to make and fly the first aircraft the world ever knew when most scientists of their time did not think it was possible. An instructive and elaborate account of that daring move was reported in Los Angeles Times, September 10, 1908 edition, culled below: "Orville Wright is the hero of the wonder-working,
fast-developing world of aeronautics tonight."- Eudora Welty

Three days ago it was Jean de la Grange, the

Frenchman, who only briefly has held his title above the Wright brothers. Twice today Orville Wright, with his aeroplane at Fort Myer, doubled the record made by De la Grange in France. This evening he broke his own record of the early morning, a sustained flight of57m. 31s, by flying for 1h. 2m.Immediately following the second record-breaking feat Wright established still another record. He took aboard as his companion Lieut. Lahm of the Signal Corps and circled the parade ground six times, descending safely after a flight lasting seven minutes. At no previous public exhibition has an aeroplane carrying two persons flown farther than a few hundred yards nor remained in the air more than a minute or two.

Your vision will make you dare to be different from others in your generation, family background and environment.

There is something fresh and new in every vision God imparts to men. You need not copy anybody if You have a vision for living.

UNAWARE OF ACHIEVEMENT

Wright made his forenoon flight unheralded, and so had a choice audience of not much more than twenty persons. He did not know how extensively he had smashed world records when he descended after circling the drill ground fifty-seven times and attaining a speed of thirty-eight miles an hour. When he learned how close he had come to flying for a full hour, he was a bit grieved. He could just as well have stayed up twice as long, but he was afraid his engine would get overheated. Examination showed it was in just as good condition as when the flight began.

News of the achievement and the report that an attempt was to be made to surpass it penetrated official circles and aroused at once an interest not before shown since the experiments with the Baldwin dirigible and the more sensational heavier than-air machine invented by the Wrights, were begun at Fort Myer. A tent-fly was stretched near the aeroplane's anchorage to shelter Secretary of War Wright and his party from the sun's rays during the exhibition, but it never was used by Gen. Wright. The latter after inspecting the strange contrivance that somewhat resembled a collection of awnings fastened together, with wires and chains with an engine and a cylinder that looked like a White head torpedo occupying a central place, stood out in the sun in front of the crowd of spectators and never for an instant took his eyes from the machine during its flight of sixty-two minutes.

When you refuse to give up your quest as a result of the vision that is burning in your heart, you will eventually climb up the ladder of success and make a lasting impart in your generation. Many people give up on their dreams quickly because of the fierce opposition they are confronted with in their pursuit. Every opposition you confront in the delivery of your vision is a spring board that is taking you closer to your mark. Surmount every seeming obstacle and take the price of your resilient pursuit.

This is the first assignment of a visionary leader to change people's orientation or perspective about life and about themselves.

When people buy into your vision, they will leave everything else to follow you.

AIR PROBLEM SERVED

'The problem of flight in the air is solved,' was the declaration made by General Murray, chief of artillery of the army, as he looked skyward and viewed the movements of Mr. Wright's machine.' The utility of the machine is to be worked out. 'He added:

"It was suggested to Gen. Murray that an experiment be made as to the feasibility of launching a shell from an aeroplane. The method suggested was to have Mr. Wright soar over an outline of a battleship which could be reproduced on the drill grounds and while over it to drop a sandbag."That would be worth trying," said the general."When the Signal Corps gets the machine we will probably undertake some experiments of that sort."As Capt. Fournier, the French military attaché, surveyed the operations, he declared with much enthusiasm:"Marvellous; I have great admiration for the work of Mr. Wright."Today's time and distance will be accepted as official by the Aero Club of America as August Post, its secretary, already has approved them. The Wright brothers' next best previous time was 38m and 36s made in a flight at Dayton in October, 1905. This flight was made by Wilbur Wright." For the Wright brothers, their vision became so daring as to break an existing world record and later to pull together the largest gathering of most notable people from all walks of life in the United States of America.

I am yet to see a man of vision static in life.
Vision produces motion because it is a force in the heart of man.

STEP OUT ON WATER!

How daring are you with your vision? Are you willing to step out on water as Peter did?

"And in the fourth watch of the night Jesus went unto them, walking on the sea. And when the disciples saw him walking on the sea, they were troubled, saying, It is a spirit; and they cried out for fear. But straightway Jesus spake unto them, saying, Be of good cheer; it is I; be not afraid. And

Peter answered him and said, Lord, if it be thou, bid me come unto thee on the water. And he said, Come. And when Peter was come down out of the ship, he walked on the water, to go to Jesus."
Matthew 14: 25-29

Peter needed only one word from the Master for a daring move. When the zeal of our vision submits to Christ's command, we shall be able to do the most impossible thing in life and our adventures would be unparallel in the world. Vision makes its possessor so daring as to do what natural laws don't support.

It is against natural laws for humans to walk barefooted on water. This was made possible because Christ was involved in the entire venture. You can only tell how to start out the adventures of your vision, how far it will take you, you cannot tell. Dare to be daring with your vision!

5 How To Communicate Your Vision

"Great speakers are not born, they're trained."
- Dale Carnegie

"Communication - the human connection - is the key to personal and career success."
- Paul J. Meyer

Communication is the human connection according to Paul Meyer. It connects leadership and followership towards achieving their goal. It connects the boss and his subordinates in the interest of an organization's objective. It connects parents and children in a family circle for peace and unity to reign. Communication connects husband and wife for love to thrive. It connects the gospel minister and his congregation to a singular vision.

Communication is the link that keeps the human circle in constant motion. In all its forms as mass communication; interpersonal communication and intra personal communication, communication holds humans together in an unbreakable union. Every culture has its unique communication system that keeps it alive and ongoing. A gospel minister must learn this and adapt to the culture of communication in the environment of his gospel work to succeed on his mission.

This is why Dale Carnegie's statement above that communicators are trained and not born - complements that of Paul Meyer. You can be trained for effective communication. There is never a skill too hard to acquire if you show enough interest and commitment to acquiring it. Learning the rudiments of communication is very essential to the gospel minister. It is the only means of passing his vision across to the people to gain their support and loyalty. Communication gap between a pastor and his congregation leads to poor assimilation, poor listening habit and eventual disconnect with the pastor's vision.

A disconnect between the pastor and his congregation often leads to confusion or pursuit of different objectives by the same group of people. A problem like this could become the pre-occupation of the pastor to the detriment of his vision. Effectively communicating a vision to the followership is a key to success at all levels of leadership positions.

Experiences have shown that where much loyalty, support and active participation are expressed by followership to leadership, communication between the two entities is usually effective, simple and dynamic. Poor communication could lead to loss of vision among the followers. A pastor's vision must be clearly stated and emphasized to his congregation if he wants the people to move at his pace.

A visionary leader gets people aligned with his vision. Until they see what you have seen, they can never become part of your pursuit!

I reiterate the vision of my ministry to get everyone involved. I make our destination clear from the outset. I repeat it enough to register it in the subconscious minds of those who hear me. In spite of what we are facing; what we are passing through; I dare to declare to them that I know who I believe and I am persuaded that nothing will stop or pull me back from fulfilling the vision he has given me! When a vision is not communicated, it dies of loneliness. Every visionary must find a most effective way of passing his vision to his followers. In doing this, the peculiarity of the environment, the social status of his followers, the existing laws around him, the culture of the people, and level of language usage must be considered. Every good vision must pass to posterity through effective communication process.

WHAT IS COMMUNICATION?

Communication scholars define it as the process of sending a message from a source, through a channel, to a receiver with the aim of getting a feedback.

Although these scholars choose different words

to express themselves, I have found out that the above definition contains the basic elements across their ideas. Therefore, every communication has source.

The pastor is the source in this case because he is the visionary. In business, the visionary is the source because the vision is original with him. Communication is said to be a process. A process is made up of series of activities. Communication is not a spontaneous thing. It is a chain reaction of steps towards a goal. Every message must be channelled through an appropriate medium to reach its audience.

The message is the vision and the medium of passing it across could be by direct or live ministration, telecast, radio, newspapers or magazines, church journals or publications, books or tracts, to mention a few. Every medium must suit the message and the receiver! The ultimate goal of any communication process is a feedback. The feedback mechanism is an essential aspect of customer relations in many corporate organizations by which they 'hear' their customers on the quality of their services. Feedback helps to check how effectively a message has been passed across. You can determine that from the people's response or reaction to the message. A followers' poor participation in a vision is an indication that the message of the vision has not been properly received.

A good preacher or leader would have to re-work his communication process all over again. The rule is the same, if the followers can see what is keeping their leader on his toes; they too will never develop duck feet! Make them see it, and they will sing it all day long. At the point of recruitment, the disciples of the Lord were introduced to the vision of their Master. That vision communicated to them became their mission. We find many examples of how vision is communicated in the Bible. Some of them are explained below.

WRITING

The art of writing is one of the oldest forms of communication. It dates back to several hundreds of years in human history. Writing is as old as the

Bible itself. In many instances recorded in the Bible, we find men and God write on the ground, on paper, in tablets of stones and on the walls with tools like fingers and ancient pen whose tip is dipped in an ink bottle to write. Writing is made a lot easier today with the advent of paper industry and pens, coupled with man's education and civilization. A vision can be communicated in writing. God told Habakkuk to write the vision He gave him for others to read it.

> *"And the LORD answered me, and said, Write the vision, and make it plain upon tables, that he may run that readeth it."*
> **Habakkuk 2: 2**

A vision clearly expressed produces action! For this reason, writing must be simple, clear and concise in communicating a vision. Writers tell us that the rule is called KISS, which means, Keep It Short and Simple! State your vision clearly and make its goal plain for anyone to understand. God told Habakkuk to make the writing plain so that it can produce the action of running in those that read it. The use of obscure and difficult language in communicating a vision could kill the vision itself. If no one understands it, you become the only burden bearer of your vision; and soon, very soon, you will break down, depressed or discouraged.

SPEECH DELIVERY

The art of public speaking is gaining popularity by the day. It underscores the importance of communication in human society. You can therefore pass your vision across through speech delivery or speaking. Speaking is the oldest form of communication. Man first spoke before he learnt to write.

I know some communication scholars who recognize thinking as a form of communication would argue that man first thought his ideas before speaking them. To them, thinking is the oldest form of communication. Well, since the aim of this book is not to achieve academic argument, let's leave all that aside. I am concerned with the forms of communication suitable as vehicles for vision transfer. I have learnt from communicators that thinking is an intra-personal communication. Since it is all about an individual the source, the channel, the message, the receiver and the feedback are all in one, I am giving little attention to that here for the benefit of our discourse. The Bible is full of speakers. God began the process by first speaking in Genesis. After He created a communication environment around Adam, the first man in the world looked at the woman and expressed his passion

"This is the bone of my bone, the flesh of my flesh. You shall be called a woman because you were brought out of man!"

Through speaking, Adam named everything in Eden his world at that time. We then understand speaking as a means of man's interaction with his world and with fellow humans. The very commission of Moses to the task of liberating Israel made him a speaker. The vision to free Israel was communicated to Pharaoh and to the children of Israel through speaking. To Pharaoh, the message was *"Let my people go..."* and to Israel, the message was

"The God of your fathers have seen your affliction and He is willing to now set you free."

Bad leadership is a product of leadership without vision.

Speaking is two directional in this case. Something you can't find in the art of writing. You must declare your vision and mission to the enemies so that they can give way and you must declare the same to the people so that they can have hope and key into your vision. If the enemies have not fled from you, maybe it's because you have not declared your mission and vision to them. Other forms of communication we find in the Bible include singing and dramatization. The messages in the songs of our choir can reiterate our vision. The drama group of the church can uphold the church's vision through playlette or drama.

A visionary leader has a benchmark, a blueprint towards which his activities are directed.

A visionary leader helps people to discover their worth, talents and potentials.

He sees in them what they don't even see in themselves.

MAKING YOUR VISION TO WORK

There are several ways to make your vision work. Just a few of them below:

1. Brainstorming: To brainstorm means to think very deeply about something as to come up with ideas on it. Brainstorming on your vision means thinking creatively about it to evolve ways of working it. A vision is a sublime substance, brainstorming brings it to the concrete level. Consider the materials you need to make the vision a reality. Ask yourself 'How do I achieve my vision?' You can go anywhere from anywhere. There is no point of limitation in life. You can make money from home. God did not create you to be limited. Tell yourself that you will make it. Consult; rub minds; and share your dreams. You need to brainstorm on how to work your vision.

2. Establish Your Strategy: Specific steps should be taken. Determine what to do in order to achieve your goal. Live within your vision. Don't pilot your vision, let the vision pilot you. It takes discipline to maintain your vision.

3. **Set Out A Date To Start:** It is never too late to start until you are late to start. It is never too late to start something new. Joyce Meyer said 'Do the hard thing first.' Every vision has a time frame.

4. **Work On Your Plans:** Once you set a date and establish your strategies, get to work. Don't allow the goal to die on the committee planning table.

5. **Evaluate The Result As You Make Progress:** Look at the positive and the negative sides. Consider what needs to be changed and what works very well.

6. **Pray Through:** Nothing moves without am over. The greatest force to move God and man is prayer. Pray your way through to your breakthrough! Never too late to start! There are people never to meet and those never to miss. You can become anything. Ask for divine empowerment.

6 Vision And Appointed Time

"... Write the vision, and make it plain upon tables, ... for the vision is yet for an appointed time, but at the end it shall speak, and not lie: though it tarry, wait for it; because it will surely come, it will not tarry." **Habakkuk 2: 2-3**

Every vision from God has an appointed time for its fulfilment. The time of fulfilment maybe short, medium range or long. Once you are sure your vision is God-given, pursue it with all the resources of God at your disposal and wait for the time of its fulfilment. Throughout the Bible, we find examples of visions tied to a specific time or calendar in God's schedule. The vision to liberate Israel from the bondage of Egypt was tied to the end of 400 years. It was one of the cases of visions whose time of fulfilment spanned over a very long period. However, at the end of it all, the vision began to speak.

God gave Abraham the vision of becoming the head of a human generation of faithful devotion and service to God after his personal example of faith and godliness. But this man was childless and age was not on his side. It went on with him like that for a while until God told him that he should expect divine visitation' According to the time of life,' which made his waiting period exactly 25 years. Either short, of medium range or long, there is usually a time of waiting for a vision to speak. From the example of Abraham, I call this period a period of active waiting in expectation. This is what makes a man of vision different from other men in the world. Waiting is either active or passive. Active waiting, as Abraham exemplify is a process of engagement with meaning and carefully selected activities in expectation of something else to come.

You cannot fold your arms and wait for your vision to speak. It just won't speak. It is only a "Deaf and dumb vision" that does not require active waiting. A deaf and dumb vision does not require any meaningful activity to aid its fulfilment. Of course, there is nothing to fulfil in a vision like that. Since it does not hear; it is certainly not going to speak. During the period of Abraham's active waiting, he was engaged in consistent prayer, kept his faith growing, endured trials, managed his private business and retained his obedience to God. That is why I describe the 24 years of his waiting as active waiting period. The fact you are so sure of your vision will make you continue to pray because you need to stay in touch with God to see the vision manifest. Prayer is the life wire that keeps you in touch with God. While actively waiting for your vision to speak, grow your faith. Smith Wigglesworth said "to remain at the same spiritual level in two days is dangerous."

The starting point of your vision is your faith in God. You need faith to see the vision actualised and you still need faith to keep the vision alive. The greater part of this faith develops during your active waiting period. Faith does not just come; the word of God births and fuels it. Apart from the word, faith and prayer grow through the trials we have to endure. Everyman's faith life is in proportion to the trials he has to endure.

The world's greatest prayer warriors endured the worst opposition to their faith and vision. Whatever you can lay your hands upon while waiting for your vision to speak, go ahead and do it. Anything legitimate; anything allowed by God that could engage your hand and your mind is worthwhile during your active waiting for your vision to speak. Abraham was waiting for God's time and was preoccupied with managing his personal business which later became the heritage of Isaac. Paul was busy with tent making while waiting for the next opening for his missionary work.

The proceed he raised from this legitimate business became part of the offerings to help some poor saints in the region of his missionary work. Get engaged with anything that can contribute positively to your life. Engage yourself with reading, studying and legitimate transactions. The knowledge, experience and proceeds from these could serve to help your vision in the end.

Obedience to divine instructions will be required throughout this period. It may be obedience through compliance with a restraining order such as when Isaac was restrained from going into Egypt. Obedience may be in the form of paying utmost price of sacrificing the most valuable thing in our lives. Any form it takes, obedience is always required during the period of active waiting for vision fulfilment.

> **Every vision from God has an appointed for its fulfilment. This time of fulfilment may be short, of medium range or long.**
>
> **A deaf and dumb vision does not require any meaningful activity to aid its fulfilment. Of course, there is nothing to fulfil in a vision like that. Since it does not hear; it is certainly Not going to speak**

WHEN THE TIME COMES

It is of interest to know when the time of a vision

comes. Every vision has a right and wrong timing. If you don't know how to discern the right time for your vision, wrong timing can lead to either of the following or both:

§ Failure
§ Defeat

Taking a close look at the example of Moses reveals so much about what happens when a vision is ill timed. Somehow, he was aware that he was born to liberate Israel from Egypt but he had no idea about the right time for this great mission. For his ignorance of God's timing, he set to go about it his own way at his own time. He relied basically on his influence as a prince in Egypt, his physical energy and knowledge of the palace life.

A vision whose time has not yet come will lack there sources to actualise it. Securing the freedom of Israel from Egypt was going to take divine intervention, divine enablement, divine method and the right time. A man of God said 'God's work done in God's way at God's own time will not lack God's resources. 'Our education is good;

it is often helpful in the pursuit of vision. Through education, we understand people, specific issues and our environment better. But in pursuing the fulfilment of a vision, it takes more than mere education. God must be involved and His time must be clear to us. Moses education at the palace alone was not enough to accomplish his vision.

Everything Moses thought was going to help assist his mission failed him because he was a step ahead of God. Rather than success, he failed and his intention was defeated. The result of it was that he ran into self-exile away from Egypt.

You will enjoy increase:
On the question of how to know when the right time comes, a text from
Exodus will help us. In this text, you will learn that when the time comes, there will be unprecedented increase.

> *"And all the souls that came out of the loins of Jacob were seventy souls: for Joseph was in Egypt already. And Joseph died, and all his brethren,*

and all that generation. And the children of Israel were fruitful and increased abundantly, and multiplied, and waxed exceeding mighty; and the land was filled with them."

Exodus 1: 5-7

As one of the signals to watch for in determining the timing of a vision, increase or expansion is often occasioned by God Himself. From a population of seventy souls in the nuclear and extended family of Jacob, the people increased in number that the land was not able to bear them any longer. That was increase. Population growth was important to the fulfilment of the vision to liberate Israel from Egypt. So much about that assignment depended on human population.

It might be easier to free a handful of people from Egypt; the challenge of possessing the land of promise was another issue ahead. You may recall, if you are a Bible student, that God strategically drove the Canaanites from their land for Israel to take over. His reason for doing so was very clear in the Bible. He wanted Israel's population to reach an advantage level to enable them have control over the land and the wild beasts around. Retaining some of the Canaanites was God's strategy to keep the land safe for His people.

You will enjoy favour:

Another signal to watch for is favour with men. I am going to take the example of David to drive home this point. After he was first anointed to be king over Israel, he ran into crisis for helping his nation and the constituted authority headed by Saul. He already was favoured by God but he needed to win favour with men. God's favour upon him led to his choice and anointing as king, but he needed to also win the support of the people. Further and further away from the throne, the troubles of life pushed him. It did not seem like the vision to reign over Israel was going to come to pass anymore until God gave him the signal of favour with the people. His account reads:

> *"And David perceived that the LORD had established him king over Israel, and that he had exalted his kingdom for his people Israel's sake."*
> **2 Samuel 5: 12**

David perceived that God had turned the hearts

of the people in his favour to help his reign as king over Israel. Vision speaks when God begins to give us favour with destiny helpers. The time of fulfilment of a vision is at hand when God increases our sphere of favour with people to assist us in the assignment given to us. In earlier verses of 2 Samuel chapter 5, we read that:

"Then came all the tribes of Israel to David unto Hebron, and spake, saying, Behold, we are thy bone and thy flesh. Also in time past, when Saul was king over us, thou wast he that leddest out and broughtest in Israel: and the LORD said to thee, Thou shalt feed my people Israel, and thou shalt be a captain over Israel. So all the elders of Israel came to the king to Hebron; and king David made a league with them in Hebron before the LORD: and they anointed David king over Israel. David was thirty years old when he began to reign, and he reigned forty years.
In Hebron he reigned over Judah seven years and six months: and in Jerusalem he reigned thirty and three years over all Israel and Judah."

2 Samuel 5: 1-5

The sphere of favour that David enjoyed with men increased. Before, he was in favour with the tribe of Judah over which he reigned seven and half years. But reigning over a tribe, out of the twelve tribes in Israel, was not the total vision package of God for David. That time, he only had a part fulfilment of his vision and the greater part was yet to manifest.

The differentiating factor of a vision, when it begins to speak, is that the visionary is no longer in charge of what is happening.

Somebody is reading this book whose vision is yet to fully manifest. I have good news for you: the Lord will bring you into favour with people that will help your destiny, in the mighty name of Jesus. All the tribes of Israel came to David as he reigned over Judah. They were united in purpose; they agreed to the same course; their request was one and their commitment was total just to make David king over Israel according to the original blue print of God for him. Vision is speaking when our favour level with and across men increases. I need to make a difference between favour with men and favour across men. We can say David had favour with all the men of Israel when they all came.

And the fact that every class of the Israelite pledged its support makes it clear that he enjoyed favour across their profiles. The engineers, the farmers, the elders, the priests name it in entire Israel came to David and gave him their full support to be king over Israel. His vision was speaking in very clear and loud language.

You will be remembered:
There is something else you need to understand. The people remembered the good deeds of David how he risked his life for Israel when he took the challenge to face Goliath to save Israel. They remembered that even though he was not the king over Israel, he had been playing roles that any good leader should play for his people. Vision speaks when God calls our good deeds to remembrance.

You can be sure that your time has come when those who forget you begin to remember and bless you. Your time has come when those who forget you can no longer sleep until they do that which the Lord has put in their hearts concerning you.

Joseph was remembered after a while of being forgotten by the inmate he helped. As an aid to the presidency, this inmate had opportunity and the influence to facilitate the release of Joseph especially when he discovered that he was imprisoned without trial on false allegations. But he never did! The time of his vision to rule over his father's house was yet to speak. When the time finally came, without him influencing anything, the former inmate began to blame himself for not helping this man. He suddenly remembered Joseph and his good deeds and quickly made a recommendation to the king about him.

As Joseph was imprisoned without trial, God also promoted him without following any protocol for promotion.

The differentiating factor of a vision, when it begins to speak, is that the visionary is no longer in charge of what is happening. It usually goes beyond him.

Moses knew he was no longer in charge when he stood before the head of the then world power and confidently demanded "Let my people go."David knew he was no longer in charge when he saw all Israel gather before him and gave him their vote of confidence without campaign. So to speak, he won the election to the throne by popular demand. And for Joseph, he was still in the prison when his matter came up at the presidency of Pharaoh. He had no way of influencing anything yet he was elevated to the position of a presidential aid in line with the vision he had from the beginning.

When a vision begins to speak, certain things will start happening to show the visionary that this is "The finger of God." I can confidently tell you that the increase, the open door, the increasing favour with men and women across all profiles and the debate in your favour in places of authority are very clear evidence that the vision God gave you is beginning to speak. God given vision speaks, no matter how long it seems to be silent; it speaks at last. That is there a son Habakkuk says "Wait for it..."There is an end in view. You will not wait in vain. Wait for your vision and understand when it begins to speak.

When a vision begins to speak, certain things will start happening to show the visionary that this is "The finger of God."

7 | Vision And Discipline

"The first and best victory is to conquer self."
- Plato, Greek Philosopher

Discipline is an essential requirement in the pursuit of vision. It will help you to maintain the 3Cs your vision needs to succeed. These 3Cs are:

§ Consistency
§ Clarity
§ Connection

Self conquest, according to Plato, is the first victory a visionary needs to win. Other obstacles to the fulfilment of vision are secondary. Like Pastor E. A Adeboye, the General Overseer of the Redeemed Christian Church of God, usually says that "Man is the greatest enemy of himself".

If you are praying for God to deal with your enemies, be sure you are not your own enemy because the answer to that prayer can be terrible. After the conquest of self, through the radical work of the cross in a man's life, it becomes easy to exercise the discipline to maintain consistency, clarity and connection in pursuit of vision.

HOW DISCIPLINE AFFECTS CONSISTENCY

Before looking at how discipline affects consistency, the question "What is consistency" should be considered. Consistency means to be steady on a course. It takes discipline to start and remain consistent on vision. Along the line, there are quite a number of distractions. Vision is often lost or compromised when the visionary gets busy 'here and there' to the detriment of the vision itself. An example in the Bible of a man busy here and there to the detriment of his primary responsibility is quite instructive. The story is found in 1 Kings chapter 20. Read the excerpt below:

"And as the king passed by, he cried unto the king:

and he said, Thy servant went out into the midst of the battle; and, behold, a man turned aside, and brought a man unto me, and said, Keep this man: if by any means he be missing, then shall thy life be for his life, or else thou shalt pay a talent of silver.

And as thy servant was busy here and there, he was gone. And the king of Israel said unto him, So shall thy judgment be; thyself hast decided it."

1 Kings 20: 39-40

A prophet disguised his face to pass a message across to the king. He came up with this allegory to hear the king's judgement and as soon as His Majesty pronounced the judgment, he took away his disguises and came back to the king to enforce the judgement he had pronounced. The point here is that when you are busy here and there to the neglect of your primary assignment as a visionary, your vision could be gone like the escape of that prisoner of war whose escape was caused by nothing but lack of diligent attention to him. Every change desired in life must come with some degree of consistency in pursuit of set goals. Ron D. Burton says "...change must always be balanced with some degree of consistency."Many potentially great people lost their vision for lack of consistency. They like to take after any available example even when they cannot tell where it leads. For your vision to materialize, you have to exercise the discipline of consistency. Stay on what you believe and stay on your expectation from it.

Consistency will make you to channel your energies towards the same goal. Lack of it wastes time and resources. Diversification should only be tolerated in the pursuit of vision if and when they are alternative routes to the same goal. In this case, I am talking about diversification in methodology or strategy since you can have a duplicate of your vision. Jesus was known for His outstanding and strict consistency. To the question "Are you the King of the Jews?" He answered "I am, and that is why I am born." The whole activities of the Saviours' life were tailored around His pursuit of the crown through the cross. Paul was consistent in the preaching of the gospel he received by divine revelation. He communicated the same gospel to Timothy and urged him to pass the message to others who would be able to maintain consistency on it.

Consistency is a matter of lifestyle and pursuit in view of a vision. You cannot afford to miss your steps. There must be consistency in the guiding principles of your life. You must be consistent on what you preach and believe. Warren Buffet, a notable American businessman and one of the richest men in the world is known for his consistency in business transactions.

A free online encyclopaedia describes him thus:"Warren Edward Buffett, born August 30, 1930, is an American business magnate, investor, and philanthropist. He is widely regarded as one of the most successful investors in the world. Often introduced as "legendary investor, Warren Buffett", he is the primary shareholder, chairman and CEO of Berkshire Hathaway. He is consistently ranked among the world's wealthiest people. He was ranked as the world's wealthiest person in 2008 and is the third wealthiest person in the world as of 2011. In 2012, American magazine Time named Buffett as one of the most influential people in the world. Buffett is called the "Wizard of Omaha", "Oracle of Omaha", or the "Sage of Omaha" and is noted for his adherence to the value of investing philosophy and for his personal frugality despite his immense wealth. Buffett is also a notable philanthropist, having pledged to give away 99 percent of his fortune to philanthropic causes, primarily via the Gates Foundation."That Buffet would get personally involved in any transaction worth his investment has been observed by business analysts as one of the principles behind his success. He has been consistent with this principle for years. The account of his successful investments is often linked with this principle of his life.

The same online resource material traces consistency or persistency to early hunting expedition by early men, a tradition still practised today by hunters in the Sahara region. It says: "Persistence hunting is a hunting technique in which hunters use a combination of running and tracking to pursue prey to the point of exhaustion. While humans can sweat to reduce body heat, their quadruped prey would need to slow from a gallop in order to pant.

Today, it is very rare and seen only in a few groups such as Kalahari bushmen and the Tarahumaraor Raramuri people of Northern Mexico. Persistence hunting requires endurance running running many miles for extended periods of time. Among primates, endurance running is only seen in humans, and persistence hunting is thought to have been one of the earliest forms of human hunting, having evolved 2 million years ago.

The persistence hunt may well have been the first form of hunting practiced by hominids. It is likely that this method of hunting evolved before humans invented projectile weapons, such as darts, spears, or slings. Since they could not kill their prey from a distance and were not fast enough to catch the animal, one reliable way to kill it would have been to run it down over a long distance. In this regard one has to bear in mind that, as hominids adapted to bipedalism they would have lost some speed, becoming less able to catch prey with short, fast charges. They would, however, have gained endurance and become better adapted to persistence hunting. Although many mammals sweat, few have evolved to use sweating for effective thermoregulation, humans and horses being notable exceptions. This coupled with relative hairlessness would have given human hunters an additional advantage by keeping their bodies cool in the midday heat."If you apply the same principle to the pursuit of vision, you get the same result. Like a persistent hunter, your prey is your vision; keep at the race until you are able to pin it down.

Every change desired in life must come with some degree of consistency in pursuit of set goals.

Like a persistent hunter, your prey is your vision; keep at the race until you are able to pin it down.

Consistency means to be steady on a course. It takes discipline to start and Remain consistent on a vision.

CLARITY

The second area of applying discipline is on maintaining the clarity of your vision. A cloudy sky around your vision makes its take off unsafe and its landing unpredictable. Like the flight of an aeroplane, a vision needs clarity of definition and direction to succeed. Geographers tell us that there are different kinds of clouds. Each cloud is a signal of something different from the others. When Elijah prayed for rain, he watched out for the cloud that brings water. Immediately he got a hint of its appearance, he knew the vision for a heavy downpour was already a reality. Meanwhile, geographers have classified the following clouds and what they signify.

The Encarta dictionary has this to say:' Clouds are created when moist air rises and cools and water condenses around dust particles to form tiny water droplets or ice crystals. The ten main types of clouds are classified on the basis of their shape and the height in the atmosphere at which they form. The types of clouds provide clues to atmospheric conditions.

Cirrus clouds

Form at high altitudes and have a wispy, delicate, feathery appearance (the word cirrus means "curl" in Latin). These feathers or curls are falling ice crystals being whipped away by winds. Cirrus clouds reveal the presence of moisture at great heights and may indicate an approaching storm or warm front.

Cirrostratus clouds

Are high-level sheets of transparent clouds. Their ice crystals scatter light and create a halo or thin veil around the Sun or Moon. These clouds usually indicate an approaching storm or warm front.

Cirrocumulus clouds

Are high-level clouds that appear as rows of tiny cumulus clouds with a
dappled texture. These clouds indicate unstable air and may warn of an approaching storm.

Cumulonimbus clouds

Are dark, towering piles of cumulus clouds, also known as thunderclouds or thunderheads. They bring heavy rain, hail, or snow, along with thunder and lightning and possibly tornadoes. They can extend the full height of the tropospherethat part of the atmosphere in which weather occurs.

Altostratus clouds
Are middle-level, thick gray clouds that cover the sky. Because they slightly obscure the Sun or the Moon, the clouds can appear as bright spots, but unlike cirrostratus clouds, they do not produce a halo. These clouds occasionally produce light snow or drizzle, but they are usually so high that their precipitation evaporates before it reaches the ground.

Altocumulus clouds
Are middle-level rows of large cumulus clouds that have darker undersides. Although not necessarily a warning of approaching precipitation, these clouds show evidence of unstable air and the possibility of light snow or drizzle.

Cumulus clouds
Are fluffy white clouds with rounded tops and

flattened bases. These clouds form at low levels on warm sunny days and usually signal the continuation of fair weather. They can develop into cumulonimbus clouds, or thunderheads.

Stratocumulus clouds

Form when low-level, layered stratus clouds break up into lumpy gray and white masses, or when cumulus clouds join to form a broken layer. These clouds may indicate approaching precipitation, which can range from alight sprinkle to heavy rain or snow.

Nimbostratus clouds

Are ground-hugging, low level, layered clouds bearing rain or snow. They
derive their name from the Latin words nimbus("rainy cloud") and stratus ("covered with a layer," or "spread out"). Nimbostratus clouds usually
produce rain or snow for a long period of time.

Stratus clouds

Are thick, gray, low-level clouds that hover at altitudes as low as 610 m (2,000 ft).They may produce light rain or snow that can last for several days. These clouds range from 2km above sea level to 8 km high. If you relate this to the spiritual realm, you will understand that there are layers of clouds that your vision must penetrate and survive, like the sun rays, for you to achieve success.

The higher your vision rise above the sea level of ordinary human achievements, the more the barriers it must survive to succeed. It is a wise and relevant strategy to pray against every cloud covering your vision at any level.

There are clouds of doubts, clouds of confusion, clouds of opposition, clouds of hatred, clouds of persecution, clouds of rejection, clouds of delay...as many as you can imagine.

Against each vision, there is a cloud that must be rolled away. The rolling away of these clouds around a vision makes the vision very clear and directional. You need the discipline to deal with your clouds if your vision must succeed.

**Take vision away from a leader,
he becomes worse than the worst
follower. A leader does not only know
the way;
he shows the way and walks the way.**

**there are layers of clouds that your
vision must penetrate and survive,
like the sun rays, for you to achieve
success.**

CONNECTION

You need discipline to get and remain connected to the right persons. There are destiny helpers and there are destiny destroyers. There are people you should not afford to miss in life and there people you should pray hard never to meet.

Strict discipline is needed to determine your associates. You only need friends that would help you reach your goal. Hiram was David's friend. He was committed to his vision of building the temple of God in Israel even though he was a foreign national. After the death of David, he lent great support to Solomon the succeeding

110

monarch and provided all that was needed to build the temple including the expertise of his men. You don't just run in and out of people. Every relation counts, one way or another. Otherwise, you should endeavour to make your relationships count.

The area of required discipline in your life would cover a wide range as wide as your vision requires. It may deny you of your legitimate appetite like the prophet sent to Bethel from Bethlehem-Judah. Unfortunately, the initial discipline he applied on his appetite did not stand the test of time as he later compromised and paid for it with his life. He died a most gruesome death through the attack of a lion. Discipline will help you to moderate your time and resources to suit your vision.

8 Why Vision Fail

"Failure is a detour, not a dead-end street."

- Zig Ziglar

Visions fail! This truth is quite awful but real and applicable to practical life situations. Many a visionary has died with his vision; others have totally given up on theirs. Failure is not final until you accept it to be so. You can succeed where you once failed. Among the factors responsible for failure of visions, I have endeavoured to explain a few which I believe are most common with men. If you work hard to deal with them in your life, fulfilling your vision is guaranteed.

DISOBEDIENCE

Paul gives us a hint on why visions fail. Making reference to his personal experience, the secret behind the success of his own vision, he said:

"Whereupon, O king Agrippa, I was not disobedient unto the heavenly vision":

Acts 26: 19

Disobedience to a vision is one of the reasons visions fail. You can be found disobedient to your vision under any of the following circumstances:

§ Doing part of what the vision requires
§ Doing the right thing at the wrong place
§ Doing the wrong thing at the right place
§ Doing the right thing at the wrong time

Saul, Israel's first monarch, was guilty of doing part of what his mandate required. His halfway obedience to the Lord cut short his vision of retaining the throne of Israel. Jonah was disobedient to the heavenly vision by heading in the wrong direction away from his duty post. It took God's loving chastisement to bring him back to his line of assignment for the reinstatement of his vision. You must get ready to obey your vision with respect to place, time and terms. Bishop

Oyedepo narrated his experience when he first went on inspection tour to the site of what has become Canaan land of his church and ministry world outreaches. He said:

"When I was being taken to inspect the piece of land upon which our ministry base is now built, I fought the people all the way there, because it was located right in the jungle. I said to them, "No, it cannot be here, let's turn back!"But the person who rode with me said "Let's go on Sir, we will soon be there.""Thank God there were four cars on that trip, and if we turned back then, we would cause confusion. So, we drove on.

Shortly, after, I said, "Are you sure ware not there yet?"The reply was "We are not there." "How can you come here for God's sake? What's wrong with your head?"I asked. The reply I got was "Please, let's just get there. If we don't get there and we need the people to help us find another place, they will be weary."When we got there, for formality sake, I said 'Okay, let's give thanks to God for all the efforts thus far.' We joined our hands together to give thanks to God, and the Lord said to me

"This is the place." I was the one making all the noise on the way there, but I said to the people, "God just spoke to me now, and He said, "This is the place." Everybody smiled."Canaan Land, (reputed to host the largest single auditorium in the world and one of Africa's best universities) is a product of divine correction," Bishop Oyedepo said. Continuing, he said "I was wrong, my little knowledge of geography was disturbing me, and church growth principles were influencing my thinking also.

I felt God did not know enough geography, because you can't possibly locate a church in the bush! If you are in Nigeria and you know the traffic problems in Lagos, you can't tell us to take church into the jungle."His experience makes it further clearer that those who fail in the pursuit of their vision need to check what they do against the time, place, and terms their vision requires. It's never too late to make amend!

You can only go as far
As your vision in life.

FEAR

Fear is another reason visions fail. In the middle of their voyage across the sea to the destination where the Master commanded, a dangerous storm rose against the disciples and fear gripped their hearts. Their confessions indicated that they had lost hope of survival. Fear obscures vision; it paralyses hope and demobilises action.

> *"And the same day, when the even was come, he saith unto them, Let us pass over unto the other side. And when they had sent away the multitude, they took him even as he was in the ship. And there were also with him other little ships. And there arose a great storm of wind, and the waves beat into the ship, so that it was now full.*
> *And he was in the hinder part of the ship, asleep on a pillow: and they awake him, and say unto him, Master, carest thou not that we perish? And he arose, and rebuked the wind, and said unto the sea, Peace, be still. And the wind ceased, and there was a great calm.*
> *And he said unto them, Why are ye so fearful? how is it that ye have no faith?"*
> **Mark 4: 35-40**

117

Fear and faith don't co-habit; one must leave for the other to stay. Each time you give in to fear, your faith is compromised! The disciples feared and the Lord asked them 'Where is your faith...?' Fear punctures the balloon of faith, making flight impossible. There are different kinds of fear that cause vision to fail. Some of them are:

§ Fear of danger the disciples felt endangered on the sea

§ Fear of the unknown the disciples took Jesus walking on the sea for a ghost and were great afraid

§ Fear of men converts among the Pharisees and Sadducees could not publicly declare their faith because they feared men

§ Fear of the enemy Israel under Saul bowed to the fear of Goliath and the Philistines

§ Fear of the future the Bible talks about a time when men's heart would fail them for fear of the future, not knowing what is ahead

§ Fear of rejection   Moses once feared the children of Israel might not accept him as their deliverer; he feared being rejected

§ Fear of people's faces Jeremiah was specifically told to ignore the angry, disapproving and resentful looks on people's faces if he was going to keep his vision alive

§ Fear of failure again, Moses feared he might fail to bring Israel out of Egypt if Pharaoh did not oblige his demand at once

§ Fear of inexperience   Timothy's inexperience and youthfulness was going to get him timid before more experienced and much older persons in the church he Pastored but for Paul's encouragement to him

§ Fear of poor communication skills Jeremiah and Moses were once victims of this kind of fear. Moses said he could not speak being a stammer and Jeremiah said he could not speak being a child

§ Fear of imaginary danger the sluggard imagines

a lion on his way, he therefore does not go out to work all day. These kinds of fear and many more are part of the reasons visions fail.

DERAILMENT

Derailment means to go off course or off track. The word derives from trains going off rail. In pursuit of vision, there are many derailments to avoid. They are detours or distractions that take a visionary off his vision and goal. Jesus knew He was born King of the Jews. More than that, He also knew the price He needed to pay to wear the crown of glory the Father had prepared for Him. But the Jews wanted to derail Him from the path to His glory by providing an alternative crown for Him. He promptly refused and avoided their company. The Bible records this account like this:

> *"Then those men, when they had seen the miracle that Jesus did, said, This is of a truth that prophet that should come into the world. When Jesus therefore perceived that they would come and take him by force, to make him a king, he departed again into a mountain himself alone."*
> **John 6: 14-15**

The Jews were sick and tired of the reign of Herod and the dominion of the Romans. They felt Jesus was better qualified as their king, considering the miracles He was able to perform. They drew up a plan to forcefully make Him their king but the Lord withdrew from the entire scheme. One important lesson to learn here is that people may attempt to derail us from our vision out of sincerity of their own interest. We have to consider God's interest and God's way to His objectives. Jesus was born to be King; He knew it so well that He replied the question on whether He is King of not with this words

"...Thou sayest that I am a king. To this end was I born, and for this cause came I into the world,..."
John 18: 37

Why did He not accept the offer to be made King since that was His vision and mission: to establish His kingdom and reign as King? Their offer was a derailment because it was going to take away the cross from the crown! God's way to Jesus' Kingship was the way of the cross; anything outside of this way amounted to failure of vision.

121

There is a way God has marked down for you to fulfil your vision; don't allow the opinion of men, even concerned men, to derail you from the means to the end. With God, the end does not justify the means but the means justifies the end. Go through your cross to wear your own crown!

If your vision in business is importation, exportation or dealing in certain goods or services, remain on it. Don't be lured into something else that is not part of your vision. Whatever you cannot prayerfully conceive as vision, don't even bother to pursue it. It is dangerous! In your career life, stay on your vision. Success in any career is a matter of staying on one's vision. Don't deviate into a career line simply because it is popular or simply because your friends belong there. Dare to be different with your vision. In family life, don't pattern your family after the culture of your environment. Every Christian marriage has been given a blueprint the Bible! Follow its precepts and you will have a happy home. If God has called you an evangelist, remain on your call. Whether an apostles, prophet, evangelist, pastor or teacher;

whatever is your line of ministry or areas of gifts, stay there, that is the pointer to your vision fulfilment. Stick to the message the Lord has given you. Martin Luther had just one message, so to speak, and the message was *"The just shall live by faith."* John Wesley had just one message, so to speak, and the message was *"Sanctification."* You can be your best in whatever is your pursuit or vision. Stay right where you are and stop drifting around! Refuse to be derailed through:

§ Carnal comparison
§ Wrong partnership
§ Wrong advice
§ Pressure of circumstances
§ Parental influence
§ Popular trend,
§ Fear,
§ Temporary difficulties,
§ Financial challenges, etc

A man was told by a minister of the gospel in Ghana that the Lord wanted him to return home to Nigeria. After the service, the man of God asked him "What do you do for a living?" He said

"I am just managing. In Nigeria, I used to sell aluminium scraps to those who make spoons, and other household tools." The man of God told him "The Lord said you should go back to Nigeria and start the business again." He did. As he got back to his business, one day, some of his scraps fell off the conveying vehicle at *Oshodi Oke,* Lagos, while in transit; and a German saw the pieces of recyclable aluminium litter the road. He packed his car, approached him and said "Who owns these?" The young man thought he's got a new customer and said "I am." The German simply gave him his card and asked him to meet him for a discussion. As he went to him, the German said "Are you ready to travel?" "To where?" he answered. "To Germany," the man said, "I've got a deal for you," he explained.

The German arranged for his visa and that was all. Today, the young man has forgotten whatever is called poverty in his life. That is the power of vision. There is a location for your vision. And whatever you do in life, do it with all your life.

ACTIVITIES OF HOUSEHOLD OR LOCAL WICKEDNESS

Joseph's vision of a glorious future would have failed but for divine intervention. The forces that wanted to cut short his vision are known as household enemies or local wickedness. Back home in Africa, people are more familiar with the activities of household enemies and local wickedness. Abroad, the closest some people get to operations of witches and wizards and other agents of wickedness is simply by watching Harry Porter series! What Harry Porter series teach on covens of wickedness are common, everyday experiences in many African homes.

Joseph's brothers hated him for his vision. They plotted to kill him and later sold him into slavery. These men represent forces of wickedness from one's household, family background or locality. The most dangerous aspect of a plot like this is when the enemies go spiritual. If the enemy is running after you with a gun, you call the police. That is the practice especially in the Western world. But there are enemies that are better equipped than the police whose weapons are invisible! You can only pray to overcome them through the provision of the cross of Jesus Christ! Physically, such enemies would eat and drink with their targets or victims, yet spiritually, they are behind his ill luck, mysterious sicknesses and diseases, barrenness, financial hardship, retrogression, addiction to evil habits, and so and so forth. Many people are unable to live and fulfil their vision because of the activities of local wickedness against them.

There is need for ferocious prayer to deal with them. Your faith must be uncompromising because they are determined too to make nonsense of the most glorious destiny. The kind of prayer required to break the oppression of local or household wickedness is what Dr. D. K. Olukoya describes as acidic prayer, offered with holy madness or holy anger. It is a no-retreat-no surrender kind of prayer. You must pray until something happens to you and to them. To them, their arms must be broken off your vision; and to you, you must find your compass and set smooth sail!

LAZINESS

A brilliant vision can fail through sheer laziness. Every genuine vision is a call to commitment and hard work. With His vision burning unquenchably in His heart, Jesus said:

> *"...My Father worketh hitherto, and I work."*
> **John 5: 17.**

Vision makes you to work. One of the direct products of vision is work. You cannot be a man with a vision and be lazy. It is impossible. The desire of a lazy visionary cannot be granted. You must work your vision to fruition.

> *"The soul of the sluggard desireth, and hath nothing: but the soul of the diligent shall be made fat."*
> **Proverbs 13: 4**

Laziness produces procrastination. A lazy man hardly finds time to do what he ought, he always feel there is a better time to come and ends up doing nothing. Laziness is sometimes not about doing nothing at all; it is about being busy with nothing meaningful to one's life. Laziness also means putting in less effort than required. A lazy student would postpone doing his home work until he has no time for it anymore. He won't read; if he does, he reads far less than he should and obtains poor grade as a reward. One of the hardest works to do is the ministry. A lazy minister of the gospel cannot fulfil his vision; not in his wildest imagination. Crave for perfection is one of the ways people grow lazy.

They want the best; they end up with nothing. They are so afraid of making a mistake; they end up not lifting a finger. The quickest way to forfeit a vision is to grow lazy. Paul the apostle was not disobedient to the heavenly vision; he worked his way to the glorious end of his career. On one of the occasions of his personal assessments in comparison to the labour of other apostles, he said:

> *"But by the grace of God I am what I am: and his grace which was bestowed upon me was not in vain; but I laboured more abundantly than they all: yet not I, but the grace of God which was with me."*
>
> **1 Corinthians 15: 10.**

"Be ye not unequally yoked together with unbelievers: for what fellowship hath righteousness with unrighteousness? and what communion hath light with darkness? And what concord hath Christ with Belial? or what part hath he that believeth with an infidel? And what agreement hath the temple of God with idols? for ye are the temple of the living God; as God hath said, I will dwell in them, and walk in them; and I will be their God, and they shall be my people."

2 Corinthians 6: 14-16

WRONG PARTNERSHIP

Your vision for a happy home, successful business, glorious career, great ministerial work or dignified future can be elusive through wrong partnership. The Bible calls wrong partnership unequal yoke and strongly forbids Christians from signing up for it in marriage, business or any area of life. The Bible says:

Wrong partnership is described in the Bible with strong words as:
§ Being unequally yoked

§ Fellowship
§ Communion
§ Concord
§ Part
§ Agreement

Each of these words indicates a strong tie, pact or unity between two parties. In marriage, you cannot marry an unbeliever; it is unscriptural. In business, you cannot get into deep agreement with an unbeliever. You will always have to do with them though, but you can wisely avoid getting into a deep agreement with them because they could and, of course, will fail you. Abraham's partnership with Lot delayed the fullness of his blessings.

As soon as God arranged the circumstance to separate the two, the Lord told him to see and possess in faith, the land He had been talking about since his call. Wrong partnership will deny you of seeing the light of your vision. And when you cannot see, you are about to walk in darkness, fumbling and stumbling along the way.

LACK OF PLAN

Without a good and workable plan, purpose will be defeated and vision will fail. Vision is like an object on the rooftop, plan is the ladder to reach it. Lofty and noble visions have died miserable deaths for lack of plan. A plan is a roadmap to fulfilling a vision. Planning is a process; it involves series of activities of goal setting, strategising and drawing up time frames to achieving them.

A good plan must have a goal to accomplish and consider the resources to accomplish the goal. Some of these resources maybe human or material, any good plan must factor in everything needed to make a vision succeed. Your plan must include performance expectations by which continuous assessment of activities would be done.

A good plan tells us where we are against where we are going and the things needed to be done to get there. Jesus says no man goes to war without first considering his resources against the army of the enemy. In other words, no man goes to war without first planning for it. For your vision to succeed, you must draw up a good plan and systematically follow it. A planned vision don't die young. Put him in a pit and he will convert it into an agricultural field. Men of vision don't allow anything to hinder them. John the Baptist had his parish in the wilderness yet he pulled crowd of listeners and converts.

Why? He stayed on his vision; he was a voice and he remained so. He drew up plan of daily ministration by Jordan River and his ministry excelled. A man of vision is awake when others are sleeping. You won't achieve anything if you don't think and plan. Do you have personal goals for your children, business and other activities in which you are engaged? Attend to your vision, give your vision whatever it takes, guard your vision, mind your vision and keep your vision.

**There is no vision
Without an enemy.**

www.ingramcontent.com/pod-product-compliance
Lightning Source LLC
Chambersburg PA
CBHW060803050426
42449CB00008B/1509